THE POWERS
OF THE
SUPREME COURT

The statue, *In Contemplation of Justice*, stands
outside the Supreme Court Building in Washington, D.C.

Cornerstones of Freedom

The Story of
THE POWERS OF THE SUPREME COURT

By R. Conrad Stein

Great Seal of the
United States of America

 CHILDRENS PRESS®
CHICAGO

Nine justices sit on the Supreme Court. From left to right in the first row are: Associate Justices Thurgood Marshall, William J. Brennan, Chief Justice William H. Rehnquist, Byron R. White, and Harry A. Blackmun. Associate Justices Antonin Scalia, John P. Stevens, Sandra Day O'Connor, and Anthony Kennedy are standing in the second row.

Library of Congress Cataloging-in-Publication Data

Stein, R. Conrad.
    The story of the powers of the Supreme Court/by R. Conrad Stein.
        p.   cm. — (Cornerstones of freedom)
    Summary: A brief overview explaining how the Supreme Court is the ultimate interpreter of our Constitution.
    ISBN 0-516-04721-3
    1. United States. Supreme Court—Juvenile literature.
2. Judicial power—United States—Juvenile literature. [1. United States. Supreme Court.   2.   Judicial power.]   I.   Title.
KF8742.Z9S74   1989   89-15885
347.73'26—dc20   CIP
[347.30735]   AC

Chambers of the Supreme Court

Reporters and photographers jam the corridors of the Supreme Court on the morning an important decision is to be announced. Decisions made by the black-robed men and women of the Court affect the everyday lives of all Americans.

The Supreme Court has nine members (one chief justice and eight associate justices), all of whom are appointed by the president. It has authority over Congress, over state legislatures, and even over the president himself. In fact, decisions made by the Supreme Court affect businesses, churches, schools and even the private lives of American citizens. Because its decisions have such an impact on the nation, the Supreme Court is a very powerful body.

The powers of the Supreme Court are rooted in the Constitution of the United States and in the

THREE BRANCHES OF GOVERNMENT

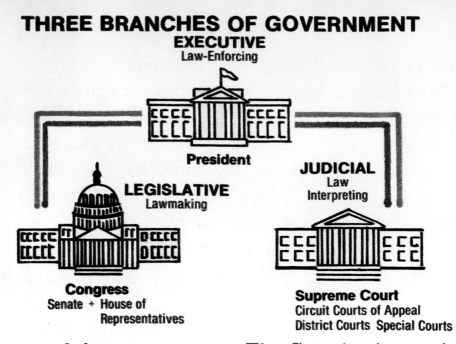

EXECUTIVE
Law-Enforcing

President

LEGISLATIVE
Lawmaking

JUDICIAL
Law Interpreting

Congress
Senate + House of Representatives

Supreme Court
Circuit Courts of Appeal
District Courts Special Courts

nature of the court system. The Constitution, written more than two hundred years ago, provides a set of rules for running the government. The Constitution divides the nation's government into three branches: the executive, the legislative, and the judicial. The executive branch is headed by the president, who is responsible for enforcing laws. The legislative branch is made up of the Congress, which has the authority to make laws and to collect money through taxation. The writers of the Constitution gave little political muscle to the judicial branch, saying, "The judicial power of the United States shall be vested in one Supreme Court..." But courts are created to settle disputes between individuals or organizations. This ability to resolve disputes is the source of the Supreme Court's power.

Through its long history, the Supreme Court has risen from humble beginnings to become one of the mightiest institutions of government. The Court's development is highlighted by important cases and famous justices. The cases are known by the names of the parties involved. If Mr. Jones sues Mr. Brown, the case will be called *Jones v. Brown.* If Mr. Jones decides to sue the federal government, the case might be called *Jones v. United States.* Disputes are heard by all the members of the Supreme Court, and the justices put their conclusions in writing. These written opinions have molded the practice of American law.

John Marshall

The master builder of the Supreme Court was John Marshall, who served as chief justice from 1801 to 1835. Though he grew up poor and was largely self-educated, John Marshall possessed a brilliant legal mind. In 1803 Marshall heard arguments in a dispute between William Marbury and President-to-be James Madison. The dispute centered on job-seeking and party politics. What seemed to be a mild squabble between politicians, however, became the most important case in American history. In *Marbury v. Madison*, the Supreme Court, for the first time ever, struck down an act of Congress on the grounds that the act violated the Constitution of the United States.

James Madison

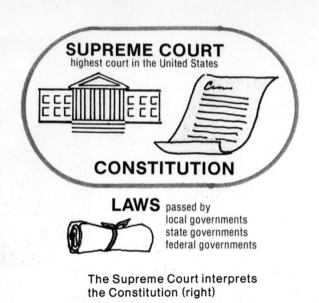

The Supreme Court interprets
the Constitution (right)

Writing his opinion in *Marbury v. Madison*, Marshall argued that the Court had the right to interpret the wording of the Constitution. "If two laws conflict with each other, the courts must decide on the operation of each," wrote the chief justice. This ability to examine acts of Congress and determine whether or not they follow the rules laid down by the Constitution is called "judicial review." Today judicial review is looked upon as a historic right of the Supreme Court. As Charles Evans Hughes (chief justice from 1930 to 1941) once observed, "We are under a Constitution, but the Constitution is what the judges say it is."

John Marshall believed the Constitution gave the federal government great authority over the states, and he used the Court to promote that belief. In the

1810 case *Fletcher v. Peck*, Marshall declared an act of a state legislature unconstitutional because it conflicted with federal power. In *McCulloch v. Maryland*, in 1819 the Marshall Court said Congress had "implied powers," meaning powers in addition to those specifically granted to it by the Constitution. In the steamboat case, *Gibbons v. Ogden*, the Supreme Court gave the federal government the right to regulate commerce between the states. John Marshall also ruled that Robert Fulton, engineer and inventor of the steamboat, could not claim exclusive rights to operate his boats on the Hudson River. These rights did not belong to him.

Robert Fulton (right) and his steamboat, *Clermont* (above)

Chief Justice Roger B. Taney (left)
and Dred Scott (above)

After John Marshall's death President Andrew Jackson named Roger Taney to be chief justice of the Supreme Court. Taney served for 28 years. Like Marshall, Taney used the Court to build the power of the federal government. During the successive terms of Marshall and Taney—a span of 62 years—the Supreme Court gained much of the authority and the prestige it has today. Though Taney was an outstanding chief justice, history will always remember him for the 1857 case *Dred Scott v. Sandford*, the most disastrous decision ever handed down by the Supreme Court.

Dred Scott was a Missouri slave who lived with his master for a brief period in Illinois and the Wisconsin Territory. Upon returning home, Scott

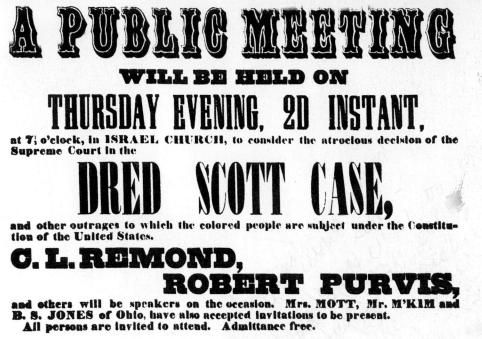

A PUBLIC MEETING

WILL BE HELD ON

THURSDAY EVENING, 2D INSTANT,

at 7½ o'clock, in ISRAEL CHURCH, to consider the atrocious decision of the Supreme Court in the

DRED SCOTT CASE,

and other outrages to which the colored people are subject under the Constitution of the United States.

C. L. REMOND,
ROBERT PURVIS,

and others will be speakers on the occasion. Mrs. MOTT, Mr. M'KIM and B. S. JONES of Ohio, have also accepted invitations to be present.
All persons are invited to attend. Admittance free.

Poster for an antislavery rally

sued for his freedom, arguing that he should have been set free once he left the slave state of Missouri and entered Illinois and the Wisconsin Territory, where slavery was forbidden. The lawsuit went to the Supreme Court, where Taney and the other justices made two fateful declarations. First, the Court said Scott was "property"; therefore he was not an American citizen and not entitled to sue in the courts. Secondly, the Court claimed Congress had no right to prohibit slavery in territories such as Wisconsin that were not yet states. The Dred Scott decision infuriated the nation's antislavery forces and was a major factor leading to the bloody Civil War. A happier ending to the drama greeted the slave Dred Scott. Two months after the court decision, Scott was given his freedom by a new owner.

After the Civil War, the states that left the Union were governed by the rules established by a Reconstruction Committee (left). They gave the newly freed male slaves the right to vote (right).

No conflict divided the nation so severely as did the Civil War. When the guns were finally stilled, Congress imposed the "Reconstruction" program on the defeated southern states. Reconstruction allowed the newly freed slaves to vote and to hold government office. In the 1870s southern whites regained political power and passed a series of anti-black measures. Laws prohibited blacks from voting or attending school with whites. "Color lines" were drawn, separating white and black seating areas on railroad cars and in public buildings. In 1896 a black Louisiana man named Homer Plessy was arrested for sitting in a "white only" railroad car. Plessy

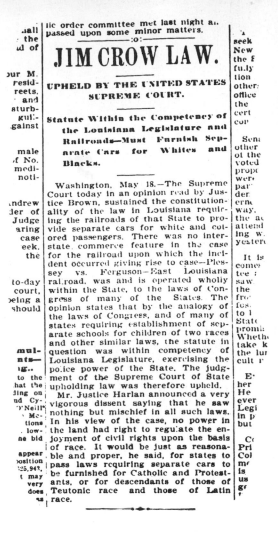

JIM CROW LAW.

UPHELD BY THE UNITED STATES SUPREME COURT.

Statute Within the Competency of the Louisiana Legislature and Railroads—Must Furnish Separate Cars for Whites and Blacks.

Washington, May 18.—The Supreme Court today in an opinion read by Justice Brown, sustained the constitutionality of the law in Louisiana requiring the railroads of that State to provide separate cars for white and colored passengers. There was no interstate commerce feature in the case for the railroad upon which the incident occurred giving rise to case—Plessey vs. Ferguson—East Louisiana railroad, was and is operated wholly within the State, to the laws of Congress of many of the States. The opinion states that by the analogy of the laws of Congress, and of many of states requiring establishment of separate schools for children of two races and other similar laws, the statute in question was within competency of Louisiana Legislature, exercising the police power of the State. The judgment of the Supreme Court of State upholding law was therefore upheld.

Mr. Justice Harlan announced a very vigorous dissent saying that he saw nothing but mischief in all such laws. In his view of the case, no power in the land had right to regulate the enjoyment of civil rights upon the basis of race. It would be just as reasonable and proper, he said, for states to pass laws requiring separate cars to be furnished for Catholic and Protestants, or for descendants of those of Teutonic race and those of Latin race.

For a time, the Supreme Court upheld the state laws that provided for separate facilities, such as the segregated School of Freedmen in Vicksburg, Mississippi.

sued, and in the case *Plessy v. Ferguson* the Supreme Court held that the creation of "separate but equal" facilities for whites and blacks did not violate the Constitution. The Court ruling in *Plessy v. Ferguson* condemned generations of African-Americans to suffer second-class citizenship in the land of their birth.

The late 1800s and early 1900s were confident years in American history. Businesses boomed and

Women (left) and young children (right) worked long hours in coal mines and factories.

giant corporations grew wealthy. "The business of America *is* business," said one corporate millionaire. The Supreme Court seemed to agree. In case after case the Court protected the rights of corporations to run their affairs free from government regulation. Even when Congress passed laws to end the practice of child labor, the Court struck down the laws, claiming they interfered with the conduct of business. Meanwhile, children as young as ten were forced to work twelve hours a day in airless factories or in dank coal mines.

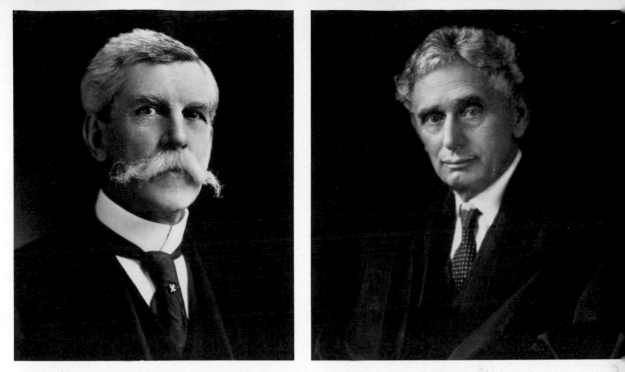

Associate Justice Oliver Wendell Holmes, Jr.   Chief Justice Louis D. Brandeis

During these confident years two justices—Oliver Wendell Holmes, Jr., and Louis Brandeis—became famous for disagreeing with the majority opinion of the Court. As a youth Oliver Wendell Holmes, Jr., thought of himself as a philosopher, and he entered the study of law reluctantly. Brandeis, on the other hand, was a lifetime crusader who championed causes favoring the poor and the underprivileged. Both Holmes and Brandeis were clever lawyers who wrote their opinions with power and wisdom. But very often the two maverick justices wrote dissenting opinions—opinions differing from those of the majority of the Court. Eventually, however, many of the minority opinions written by these "Great Dissenters" were adopted by future Courts.

President Franklin Delano Roosevelt's radio broadcasts were called "fireside chats."

The nation's industries ground to a sickening halt in the 1930s, when the Great Depression gripped the United States. One of every four workers lost his or her job, and lines of poor people waiting to buy day-old bread wrapped around city blocks. President Franklin Delano Roosevelt and a Democratic Congress passed laws designed to provide depression relief, but a conservative Supreme Court rejected many of the measures. Hoping to remake the Court with his own appointees, Roosevelt supported a law that would increase the number of Supreme Court justices from nine to as many as fifteen. The proposal was legal because the Constitution does not specify how many justices should sit on the Supreme Court. But many of Roosevelt's friends in Congress rejected the "court-packing" plan because such a law would weaken the Supreme Court and jeopardize its time-honored practice of judicial review.

President Roosevelt tried to change the Supreme Court by adding judges that agreed with his programs. This political cartoon comments on Roosevelt's plan.

I SAY HE CAN'T DO THIS TO YOU!

SENATE

SEIZURE

H.S.T.

But He's Done It

The Supreme Court overruled President Truman's seizure of the steel mills in 1952.

5¢ WEATHER
Closedy with showers Tuesday. High 74; low 54. See Page 28.
Telephone ANdover 3-4800 DEarborn 2-2223
Vol. 5, No. 106

CHICAGO DAILY SUN-TIMES
Copyright, 1952, by Field Enterprises, Inc.

FINAL

Average net paid circulation for last 6-month A.B.C. period 550,2

TUESDAY, JUNE 3, 1952
56 Pages—Two Sectio

COURT UPSETS STEEL SEIZURE: STRIKE BEGINS!

Chicago Area Plants Shut; Prolonged Walkout Seen

A crippling strike by 650,000 members of the CIO United Steelworkers, including 80,000 in the Chicago area, was shutting the nation's basic steel mills Monday night. It came when the U.S. Supreme Court ruled that President Truman's seizure of the steel industry was invalid.

Philip Murray, president of the steelworkers' union and the Congress of Industrial Organizations, declared at Pittsburgh:

"The act of the court leaves the members of the United Steelworkers without the benefit of a collective bargaining agreement. In the

NEW YORK (AP)—The steel industry announced Monday night that it is ready to resume bargaining with the striking CIO United Steelworkers.

absence of a wage agreement our members have no alternative other than to cease work."

Board Chairman Ben Moreell of Jones & Laughlin Steel Corp., the fourth largest steel company in the nation, said:

"It seems that once again wise and courageous men have come to the defense of our form of constitutional government."

A prolonged walkout was seen by Charles M. White, president of Republic Steel Corp., in Cleveland. But he added:

"The ruling of the U.S. Supreme Court vindicates the position we have taken throughout this controversy—that the seizure of the steel industry was illegal. The decision should be heartening to every freeContinued on Page 3

Court 6-3 Against Truman Government Returns Mill

WASHINGTON (UP)—The Supreme Court has overthrown President Truman's seizure of the steel industry unconstitutional. A nationwide strike of 650,000 CIO Unit Steelworkers began immediately as the mills were return to private ownership. By a 6 to 3 vote the high tribunal rul that Mr. Truman's seizure order was unconstitutional.

In the first ruling of its kind handed down by the Supreme Court, the justices decided th Mr. Truman had no power under law or by the Constitution—to order the seizure. T decision knocked down ev argument advanced by the government.

Within three hours after the cision came down at noon Mr. Truman instructed Comm Sec. Sawyer to end the government seizure "immediately." At 2:40 p (Chicago time) Sawyer announ he had so notified the steel c panies—a step which Philip Mur Steelworkers and CIO president ready had anticipated with his st call.

Simultaneously, the govern ordered an immediate halt to all liveries of steel for civilian proj

Continued on Pag

Text of majority opini in steel seizure case an abstracts of dissenting an concurring opinions will b found on Pages 17, 18 an 19.

Walking off the job at U.S. Steel's South Works, workers find pickets already on duty. Supreme Court ruling against President Truman's seizure of steel industry signaled renewal of the strike. (SUN-TIMES Photo by Dave Mann)

The president and the Supreme Court clashed again in 1952 when Harry Truman seized the nation's steel mills to prevent a strike. The Court asserted its authority over the president when it said the Constitution forbade him from seizing private property. Again in 1974 the Court exercised power over the president by ordering Richard Nixon to release taped recordings of his staff meetings to investigators probing the Watergate scandal.

In the 1950s a long string of civil rights cases began reaching the Supreme Court. The Court's decisions on these civil rights cases helped to fashion a new way of life for African-Americans.

Linda Brown

Chief Justice Earl Warren

The lawyers in the Brown case were George E. C. Hayes
(left), Thurgood Marshall (center), and James M. Nabrit (right).

For decades many states maintained separate
school systems for blacks and whites. In 1951 a
railroad worker named Oliver Brown sued the city
of Topeka, Kansas, for forbidding his daughter to
attend an all-white school in her neighborhood.
Brown was represented by the talented lawyer
Thurgood Marshall, who later became the first black
justice of the Supreme Court. In 1954 Chief Justice
Earl Warren handed down a landmark decision con-
demning school segregation. Warren first referred
to the almost 60-year-old case of *Plessy v. Ferguson*,
which held that a system of "separate but equal"
facilities for the two races was acceptable under the

Constitution. Of that doctrine Warren wrote, "We conclude that in the field of public education the doctrine of 'separate but equal' has no place. Separate educational facilities are inherently unequal."

Although the *Brown v. Board of Education of Topeka* decision made racially separate schools illegal, blacks still faced humiliating discrimination in other areas. The walls of segregation began tumbling in the 1950s, when the black-led civil rights revolution saw riders boycotting segregated buses in Alabama and students "sitting in" at all-white lunch counters in North Carolina. Spurred by the demonstrations, Congress passed a sweeping civil rights act that outlawed racial segregation in public accommodations. In a 1964 case the Supreme Court declared the new civil rights act constitutional, and forever buried the notion that separate but equal facilities were acceptable in America.

Cases involving free speech, school prayer, abortion, discrimination against women, the rights of people accused of a crime, and many other emotionally charged issues flood the Court today. The Court's decisions are hailed by some Americans and cursed by others. It is impossible for the Supreme Court to avoid controversy. As Oliver Wendell Holmes, Jr., once said of the Court's solemn chambers, "We are very quiet here, but it is the quiet of a storm center."

The Constitution guarantees Americans the right to publicly express their opinions about issues such as school prayer and abortion. In the 1960s, sit-ins at segregated lunch counters (below left) and massive marches overturned long-standing segregation laws.

An 1888 engraving showing the nine members of the Supreme Court meeting in the old Senate Chamber.

To understand the controversies that surround the Supreme Court, it is necessary to examine how it works. Since 1869 the Court has been made up of nine members. Opinions are decided by a majority. Often that majority is as slim as 5 to 4. The chief justice is considered to be the Court's leader, but he or she has only one vote. All justices are appointed by the president with the approval of the Senate. In recent years, the Senate has been harsh on Supreme Court nominees. The Senate rejected President Reagan's nominee Robert Bork in 1987. Once a justice is approved, he or she sits on the Court for life. The Constitution allows the Senate to remove a corrupt justice through the impeachment process, but that has never happened in the nation's history.

During the 1980s about 5,000 cases a year reached the Supreme Court from lower courts. In any one year the Supreme Court agrees to hear only about 200 cases. The disputes the Court is willing to consider involve the nation's most pressing problems. Groups of lawyers who represent each party in a dispute bring their arguments before the Court. For most lawyers, to present a case to the Supreme Court is the fulfillment of a lifetime dream. Proceedings are informal, and justices will often interrupt lawyers by firing questions during their arguments. Decisions are made among the justices behind closed doors. Any justice may write the majority opinion. Justices in the minority are free to write dissents.

High school group visits the Supreme Court.

A justice's opinion will be read by future generations of students and scholars. Consequently, justices work with painstaking care on their written decisions. Louis Brandeis once rewrote a single opinion 43 times. Sometimes a justice's writing will be dry and crammed with legalistic terms. Often, however, a justice will pour his soul into his opinion. Writing a dissenting opinion in a World War II case, Justice Frank Murphy said of the imprisonment of Japanese civilians, "I dissent, therefore, from this legalization of racism. Racial discrimination in any form and in any degree has no justifiable part whatever in our democratic way of life." Frequently a justice will create an example to make a point. Writing an opinion in a free-speech case, Oliver Wendell Holmes, Jr., once said, "The most stringent

During World War II, Japanese-Americans were denied their civil rights and moved to camps.

protection of free speech would not protect a man in falsely shouting *"Fire!"* in a theater and causing a panic."

Decision days—usually on Mondays—can be occasions for emotional fireworks. Reporters crowd into the courtroom on the morning a sensitive decision is to be announced. Everyone, including the justices, feels the excitement of a decision day. When the school desegregation case *Brown v. Topeka* was to be announced, Justice Robert Jackson rose from his sickbed to be present in the chambers even though he had suffered a severe heart attack just days earlier. On one decision day, Justice Felix Frankfurter read a dissenting opinion with such fire and fervor that Chief Justice Earl Warren scolded him in open court in front of the reporters.

LIBERTY BELL, 1954

The Supreme Court outlawed segregation in public schools.

NOTICE

IT IS REQUIRED BY LAW UNDER
PENALTY OF FINE OF $5.00 TO $25.00
THAT WHITE AND NEGRO PASSENGERS MUST
OCCUPY THE RESPECTIVE SPACE OR SEATS
INDICATED BY SIGNS IN THIS VEHICLE

COLORED.

A woman points to a segregation sign that once appeared on buses.

A majority opinion creates a precedent—an important legal concept. Justices use precedents as building blocks to form their opinions. Lawyers arguing before the Court cite precedents in trying to win their case. Written opinions handed down by the Court refer to precedents, some of which date back more than a century. But the Supreme Court is not afraid to act contrary to precedent and overrule itself. Scores of civil rights cases overruled *Plessy v. Ferguson*, which established the precedent that "separate but equal" facilities for the races does not violate the Constitution.

In affirmative-action suits the Court has decided cases without creating a clear precedent. Affirmative-action programs were created by Congress to give jobs and opportunities to women and minorities, groups that had suffered from discrimination. However, it has been argued that affirmative action discriminates against white males. In the late 1970s a white student named Allan Bakke was denied admission to the University of California's medical school. Bakke had higher test scores than some of the minority students who were admitted under affirmative action, and he sued the university, claiming he was discriminated against due to his race. In the Bakke case the Court compromised by declaring that he, as an individual, had suffered discrimination, but that affirmative-action programs did not violate the Constitution. As the Court enters the 1990s the issue of how affirmative action affects the rights of white males is still undecided.

Allan Bakke won his case before the Supreme Court.

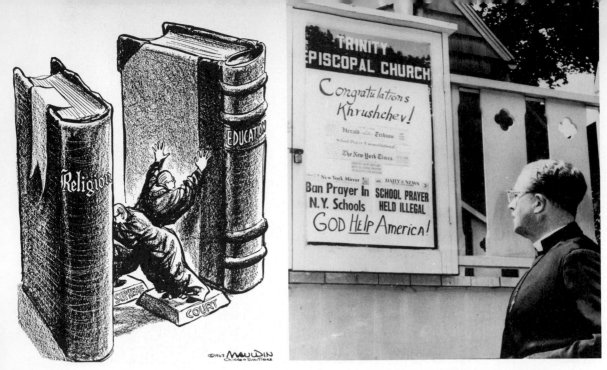

The Supreme Court is dealing with religious questions on a case-by-case basis.

In many instances the details surrounding an issue are so complicated that the Court cannot create a policy, and has to judge each dispute on a case-by-case basis. According to the Constitution, the government cannot create a state religion, and it cannot show favoritism toward any religious group. The 1962 *Engle v. Vitale* case outlawed prayer in public schools because the Court believed such prayers violated the Constitution's intent to keep church and state separate. But can a city at Christmastime display a Nativity scene with a representation of the Christ Child? Does such a display favor Christianity over other religions? In 1984, in the case of *Lynch v. Donnelly*, the Supreme Court held that a traditional Nativity scene did not

Chief Justice Earl Warren, left, was appointed by President Dwight D. Eisenhower, right.

violate the separate church and state doctrine. No doubt many more cases will come to the Supreme Court regarding the complex relationship between church and state.

Usually a president will appoint justices who share his or her own political philosophy. Once in office, however, the justice is free to act in the way he or she sees fit. President Theodore Roosevelt was so disappointed by the decisions made by his nominee, Oliver Wendell Holmes, Jr., that he said of Holmes, "That man has the backbone of a banana." In 1953 President Dwight Eisenhower nominated Earl Warren to be chief justice. Warren, the ex-governor of California, was a middle-of-the-road Republican who was expected to precisely represent

Many Americans protested the decisions of what was called the Warren Court.

Eisenhower's views. But in office Warren became a crusading liberal, and acted as the guiding force behind school integration cases. In some areas of the country Warren was so disliked that billboards appeared on highways blaring out the message: IMPEACH EARL WARREN.

The Constitution is often called a "living document" because of the way it has developed. It has had to grow with the times, because it was written by eighteenth-century men who could not imagine the problems faced by modern Americans. Keeping the Constitution alive is the sacred trust of the Supreme Court. In its efforts the Court has taken great pains to interpret the Constitution in light of changing times, but not to act as a lawmaking body. This restraint has kept the Supreme Court's respect high in the minds of the people and their elected leaders. Harvard Law School Professor Paul Freund once pointed out, "The [Supreme] Court has been careful not to read the provisions of the Constitution like a last will and testament, lest they indeed become one."

Finally, the Supreme Court is a key element in the separation of powers concept. The writers of the Constitution divided American government into the executive branch, the legislative branch, and the judicial branch, so that each branch would serve as a watchdog over the others and so that no single branch could acquire excessive power. Historically the judicial branch has acted as a referee, insisting that every department of government follow the rules laid down by the Constitution. The Supreme Court, in its role of interpreting the Constitution, has helped to preserve it. The patriot Daniel Webster once said of the Supreme Court, "The Constitution without it would be no Constitution—the government, no government."

INDEX

affirmative-action suits, 26-27
African-Americans, 10-11, 12-13, 18
Bakke, Allan, 27
Bork, Robert, 22
Brandeis, Louis, 15
Brown, Oliver, 19
Brown v. Board of Education of Topeka, 20, 25
child labor, 14
church and state, separation of, 28-29
Civil War, 11, 12
civil rights cases, 12-13, 18
Congress, 5, 6, 7, 8, 9, 11, 16, 20, 26-27
Constitution of the United States, 5, 6, 7, 8, 17, 18, 20, 22, 26, 27, 28, 30-31
discrimination against African-Americans, 12-13, 20
Dred Scott v. Sandford, 10

Eisenhower, Dwight, 29, 30
Engle v. Vitale, 28
Fletcher v. Peck, 9
Frankfurter, Felix, 25
free speech, 20, 24-25
Freund, Paul, 31
Fulton, Robert, 9
Gibbons v. Ogden, 9
Great Depression, 16
Holmes, Oliver Wendell, Jr., 15, 20, 24-25, 29
Hughes, Charles Evans, 8
Jackson, Robert, 25
Jackson, Andrew, 10
judicial review, 8, 17
lawyers and the Court, 23, 26
Lynch v. Donnelly, 28-29
Madison, James, 7
Marbury, William, 7
Marbury v. Madison, 7-8
Marshall, Thurgood, 19
Marshall, John, 7, 8, 9, 10

McCulloch v. Maryland, 9
Murphy, Frank, 24
Nixon, Richard, 18
opinion, dissenting, 15, 23, 24
opinion, majority, 15, 22, 24, 26
opinion, written, 7, 8, 26
Plessy v. Ferguson, 13, 19, 26
Plessy, Homer, 12-13
precedent, 26
president, 5, 6, 16, 18, 22, 29
Reagan, Ronald, 22
Roosevelt, Theodore, 29
Roosevelt, Franklin Delano, 16
school segregation, 19, 20
school prayer, 20, 28
Scott, Dred, 10-11
Senate, 22
"separate but equal" facilities, 13, 19-20, 26
Taney, Roger, 10, 11,
Warren, Earl, 19-20, 25, 29-30
Webster, Daniel, 31

About the Author

R. Conrad Stein was born in Chicago and graduated from the University of Illinois. He is the author of many books, articles, and short stories written for young readers. Mr. Stein lives in Chicago with his wife and their daughter, Janna.

Mr. Stein was pleased to write this book about the Supreme Court because he specialized in the study of constitutional development while in college.